THE CREATION WHICH ANTONI GAUDÍ DEDICATED HIS ENTIRE LIFE TO

THE EXPIATORY TEMPLE OF THE
Sagrada Familia

TEXTS: RICARD REGÀS / PHOTOGRAPHS: CARLOS GIORDANO & NICOLÁS PALMISANO

DOSDEARTE EDICIONES

Contents

THE ORIGINS OF ANTONI GAUDÍ'S UNIVERSAL MASTERPIECE

JOSEP MARIA BOCABELLA
DEVOTED FOLLOWER OF SAINT JOSEPH, HE PRO-
MOTED THE CONSTRUCTION OF THE TEMPLE.

01

.:a bookseller
wanted to
dedicate a great
temple to the
Holy Family...

LEFT
ELEVATION OF THE TEM-
PLE FROM ITS WEST-
FACING SIDE, DRAWN BY
THE ARCHITECT HIMSELF.

BELOW
ONE OF THE FOUR HERALD
ANGELS THAT ANNOUNCE
THE ARRIVAL OF JESUS,
POSITIONED HIGH UP ON
THE COLUMNS OF THE
NATIVITY FAÇADE.

WAITING FOR GAUDÍ

Although nobody seems to hesitate when attributing Sagrada Familia to Antoni Gaudí, the truth of the matter is that the great architect from Reus was not the author of the first project for the expiatory temple and was neither present during the first few months of building work. The origins of Sagrada Familia date back to its foundation, in 1866, of the Spiritual Association of Devotees to Saint Joseph, an organization created by a Barcelona bookseller and publisher, Josep Maria Bocabella, with the aim to revindicate the patriarchal figure of the Church, and the Catholic faith in general, during some very difficult decades for religion in Spain. A law passed in 1836, called the *Desamortización de Mendizábal,* resulted in the expropriation of many properties, land, churches, monasteries and convents, of all religious orders. The process plunged the clergy into serious economic difficulties and greatly lessened their long-standing influence on Spanish society. ↪ It is hardly surprising, then, that during this period, right from the bosom of the Church, emerged numerous figures immersed in a frenzy of missionary activity to restore the Faith of a society that, on the other hand, was undergoing radical changes brought about by the Industrial Revolution. The creation of the Spiritual Association of Devotees to Saint Joseph, which in 1878 now had more than half a million members, falls within this combative reaction of the Church and endeavours to get spirituality back into society. Bocabella, President of the Association, came up with the idea of building a temple in Barcelona dedicated to the Holy Family after visiting the religious sanctuary in Loreto (Italy), which apparently held the Holy House, Jesus, Mary and Joseph's home in Nazareth. ↪ It wasn't until 1881 that Bocabella amassed 172.000 pesetas, around 1000 euros, in order to be able →

to start construction on a site in the Eixample, the new neighbourhood planned by Ildefons Cerdà to urbanize the *Llano de Barcelona* after the destruction of the medieval walls in 1854. Even though the temple's promoter would have preferred a more central location, he made do with an area of land a kilometre and a half from Passeig de Gràcia, which still came under the municipal district of Saint Martí de Provençals, a locality later absorbed by metropolitan Barcelona in 1897. ⮞ In order to direct the work, Bocabella counted on diocesan architect, Francesc de Paula del Villar, who offered his services free of charge. In line with historicist trends prevailing at the time, he designed a neo-Gothic building whose first stone was laid on Saint Joseph's Day in 1882. ⮞ However, just a year later, Del Villar resigned from the project due to differences with the promoter but more so with the main technical advisor, the great historicist architect Joan Martorell, over choice of materials and construction methods used. Bocabella then offered actual control of the project to Martorell. The latter declined, but without a moment of doubt recommended his most talented disciple, Antoni Gaudí, who at the age of 31 took the reins of a project that would mark his entire career, convert into Barcelona's symbol and become one of the great architectonic works of the 20th century. ⮞

⮞
**THE APSE AND
NATIVITY FAÇADE**
AFTER TAKING CONTROL OF CONSTRUCTION WORK IN 1883, GAUDÍ SET UPON FINISHING THE CRYPT AND PLANNING THE TEMPLE AS A WHOLE, OPTING TO CONSTRUCT IT SECTION BY SECTION, STARTING WITH THE APSE, THE NATIVITY FAÇADE AND THE EASTERN SECTOR OF THE CLOISTER. THIS PHOTOGRAPH, TAKEN IN 1904, SHOWS THE INTERIOR SIDE OF PART OF THE APSE AND THE NATIVITY FAÇADE, WITH CORRESPONDING TOWERS STILL TO BE STARTED. THE SITE WAS LOCATED WITHIN A ZONE IN THE EIXAMPLE THAT WASN'T VERY DEVELOPED, WITH MOSTLY FACTORIES AND WAREHOUSES.

01

FRANCESC DEL VILLAR
DIOCESAN ARCHITECT OF
BARCELONA BETWEEN 1874
AND 1892. HE VOLUNTEERED
TO CARRY OUT THE PROJECT
IN 1877 AND THEN RESIGNED
FROM IT IN 1883.

**01. ELEVATION
OF DEL VILLAR'S
ORIGINAL PROJECT**
THE ARCHITECT DESIGNED A
PURELY NEO-GOTHIC STYLE
BUILDING, WITH HONEY-
COMBED WINDOWS, FLYING
BUTTRESSES AND CIMBORIO.

02. FRONT VIEW
THE NARROW BELL TOWER
OVER THE PORTICO, DECO-
RATED WITH A TAPERED
ROOF, PRESIDES OVER THE
FRONTAL ELEVATION OF
FRANCESC DEL VILLAR'S
PROJECT.

03. GROUND PLAN
DEL VILLAR DESIGNED A LAT-
IN CROSS GROUND PLAN
WITH THREE NAVES. FROM
THIS PLAN GAUDÍ ONLY CON-
SERVED THE CONTOURS OF
THE HEAD SECTION, WHOSE
FOUNDATIONS HAD BEEN
ALREADY LAID.

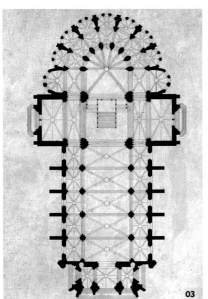

03

THE FIRST PROJECT

To start with, Josep Maria Bocabella, the temple's promoter, was keen on constructing an exact replica of the basilica that was in Loreto, Italy, whose visit gave him the idea to build an expiatory temple in Barcelona dedicated to the Holy Family. ✃ However, Francesc de Paula del Villar, the appointed architect, convinced Bocabella to rule out this option and devised a neo-Gothic building, a very fashionable style at a time dominated by the revision of past methods and based on the recuperation of constructive elements typical of the era of great medieval cathedrals: ogival arches, crossed vaults, normal buttresses and flying buttresses whose capacity to support a lot of weight allowed the construction of very high buildings with large openings in walls which light could easily flood through. ✃ Del Villar planned a church with three naves, a Latin cross ground plan, a large crypt, apse with seven chapels and an elegant bell tower over the portico that would have reached eighty-five metres high, only half the size of the highest tower in Gaudí's project. Although the scale of the building designed by Del Villar would have been inferior to that of the genius from Reus, the temple's measurements in the original project would have reached 97 metres long by 44 metres wide, which far exceeded those of the Cathedral of Barcelona. ✃

01. GAUDÍ'S TABLE

GAUDÍ WORKED IN THIS SIMPLE ROOM LOCATED IN THE WORKSHOP HE FITTED OUT IN THE TEMPLE.

02. FLIGHT TO EGYPT

A MODEL POSES SO THAT GAUDÍ AND THE SCULPTORS CAN STUDY THE FIGURE OF THE VIRGIN IN THE SCULPTURAL GROUP ON THE HOPE PORTICO, ON THE NATIVITY FAÇADE.

03. BEDROOM

IN 1925, A YEAR BEFORE HIS DEATH, GAUDÍ MOVED INTO SAGRADA FAMILIA'S WORKSHOP, SETTING UP HIS BED THERE IN A CORNER OF THE STUDIO.

04. THE FIRST STONE

THE CEREMONY OF LAYING THE FIRST STONE, ON SAINT JOSEPH'S DAY IN 1882, WAS A GRAND AFFAIR IN THE CITY. BISHOP URQUINAONA OVERSAW THE CEREMONY. GAUDÍ WAS NOT YET INVOLVED IN THE PROJECT.

05. AERIAL VIEW IN 1928

TWO YEARS AFTER GAUDÍ'S DEATH, THE NATIVITY FAÇADE'S BELL TOWERS WERE ALMOST FINISHED. THE TEMPLE'S SURROUNDINGS, AN INDUSTRIAL ZONE FAR FROM THE CITY CENTRE, WERE ALSO BEING DEVELOPED.

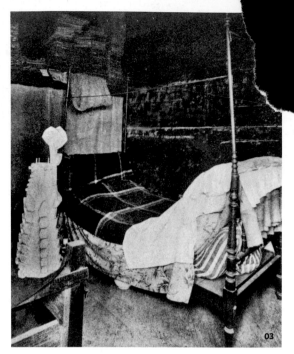

01

01. **GAUDÍ'S WORKSHOP.** IT WAS ON THE ACTUAL SITE, FULL OF MODELS AND PLASTERCASTS. **02. VISIT FROM THE PAPAL NUNCIO FROM THE VATICAN.** IN 1915, THE CARDINAL RANGONESI SAID GAUDÍ WAS "ARCHITECTURE'S DANTE". **03. THE LEAGUE.** GAUDÍ SHOWS THE TEMPLE TO MEMBERS OF THE NATIONALIST LEAGUE, THE MAJORITY PARTY IN CATALONIA AT THE START OF THE 20TH CENTURY. **04. ROYAL VISIT.** GAUDÍ WITH PRINCESS PAZ, SISTER OF ALFONSO XII. **05. ARGENTINE SOLDIERS.** VARIOUS OFFICIALS FROM THE ARGENTINIAN ARMY, IN 1924, WITH GAUDÍ AND THE POLITICIAN RAIMON D'ABADAL, IN THE FOREGROUND.

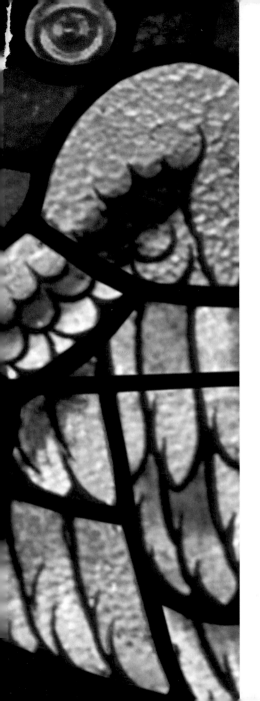

THE CRYPT, THE FIRST STEP IN A LONG PROCESS OF CONSTRUCTION

COLOUR AND ILLUMINATION
DETAIL OF ONE OF THE STAINED GLASS WINDOWS THAT DECORATE THE CRYPT CHAPELS.

...Gaudí is obliged to respect what his predecessor constructed...

AN INGENIOUS TOUCH

After Francesc de Paula del Villar's resignation from the project, Gaudí officially took over work on Sagrada Familia on the 3rd of November in 1883. He was only 31 years old and had just completed quite an important project: the Casa Vicens, a summer residence on what were then the outskirts of Barcelona. Despite Gaudí's lack of experience, Joan Martorell, his mentor, could not help but notice the energy and creativity that the young man channelled into his commissions and thus entrusted him with this enormous project. ❧ When he took on the project the subsoil had already been excavated in preparation for the crypt and the pillar beams erected. The architect would have liked to change the location of the temple and position it diagonally over the block, so with the precision of a compass the Nativity façade faced daybreak and the Passion façade towards sunset. However, this idea was not possible for budgetary reasons as work was financed by donations, and Gaudí also respected what Del Villar had planned for the location of the temple and, more concretely, for the configuration of the crypt: a total of 22 vaults supported by sturdy pillars of oval section generate a striking semi-circular area made up of seven exterior chapels, an intermediate deambulatory and a central interior area. These seven chapels, fitted into apsidioles, find their counterpoint on the opposite side of the crypt, a straight wall that holds five more chapels, one of which, the central one, is taken up by the main altar. ❧ Regarding Del Villar's original plan, Gaudí did introduce some changes. On the architectonic plan, he had a ditch dug around the crypt to favour illumination and ventilation. With the same objective, he raised the vault of the central area to install large windows that would open on to the temple's interior, below the high altar. Moreover, →

he changed the location of the access staircases, which connected the crypt with the temple and the choir galleries, situated high up on the lateral naves. As for its ornamentation, Gaudí topped the pillars with capitals carved with naturalist motifs and decorated the vaults with sculpted and polychrome keystones. ❧ The architect had been educated in a historicist academic background, the school of thought founded on the recuperation of olden and medieval ways and which left its mark on 19th century architecture. Moreover, one of his references was Eugène Viollet-le-Duc, restorer of large French medieval constructions. It is therefore quite normal that during this period he would feel quite comfortable with the neo-Gothic features left behind by his predecessor. ❧ From the start, however, Gaudí gave his own special touch to the crypt, with these changes that give the space its own indisputably Gaudían feel despite having been originally planned by another architect. On the 19th of March in 1885, about sixteen months after Gaudí had taken Sagrada Familia under his wing, the chapel devoted to Saint Joseph was established and became the first space destined for worship within the entire temple. Six years later, just before Josep Maria Bocabella's death, construction work on the crypt was deemed complete and since the year 1930 it has been used as a parish. ❧

❧
BUILDING WORK
THE THICK PILLARS IN THE CRYPT, READY TO WITHSTAND THE WEIGHT OF THE VAULTS, HALFWAY THROUGH THE 1890'S, WITH GAUDÍ AT THE HELM OF CONSTRUCTION WORK.

❧
CRYPT CROSS SECTION
DRAWING OF ELEVATION OF THE CRYPT JUST AS IT WAS DESIGNED BY GAUDÍ, WITH THE VAULT IN THE CENTRAL ZONE HIGHER THAN THE ONES IN THE CHAPELS AND DEAMBULATORY.

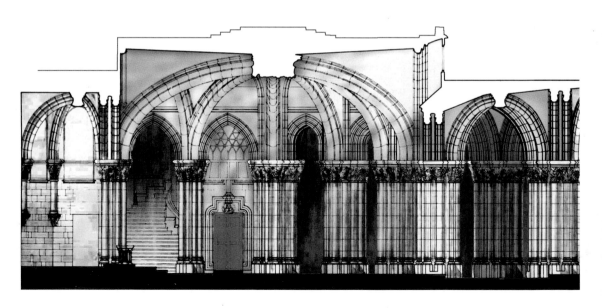

01. THE ALTAR

THE CRYPT WAS USED AS A PARISH FROM 1930. THE ALTAR WAS INSTALLED IN THE CENTRAL CHAPEL ON THE SOUTHERN WALL.

02. THE PAVING

CLOSE UP OF THE POLY-CHROME MOSAIC ON THE CRYPT FLOOR WHERE A BIRD CAN BE MADE OUT FEEDING ON A GRAPE. WHEAT, WHICH ALSO APPEARS IN THE MOSAIC, AND THE VINE ARE SYMBOLS OF THE EUCHARIST.

03. THE SACRISTY DOORWAY

FRAMED BY A FLAT ARCH-WAY, IT IS CARVED IN WOOD AND IS DECORATED WITH POLISHED STEEL.

04. THE ALTARPIECE

A WOOD RELIEF CARRIED OUT BY SCULPTOR JOSEP LLIMONA WITH A REPRESEN-TATION OF THE HOLY FAMILY PRESIDES OVER THE CHAPEL OF THE CRYPT'S ALTAR. THIS ALTARPIECE WAS ORIGINAL-LY FOUND IN THE CHAPEL OF CASA BATLLÓ, ALSO WORK OF GAUDÍ. FOR MANY YEARS, THERE WAS A COPY OF THE ORIGINAL IN THE CRYPT.

01

02

03

01

02

03

01. SAINT JOSEPH
THE CENTRAL CHAPEL IN THE APSIDAL ZONE IS DEDICATED TO SAINT JOSEPH. IT WAS THE FIRST ONE FINISHED DUE TO JOSEP MARIA BOCABELLA'S DEVOTION TO THE CHURCH'S PATRIARCH.

02. CHAPEL OF OUR LADY CARMEN
THE REMAINS OF ANTONI GAUDÍ, VERY DEVOTED TO THIS VIRGIN, ARE FOUND IN THIS CHAPEL, BELOW A SOBER TOMBSTONE.

03. CHAPEL OF SAINT CHRIST
IN THIS SPACE ARE THE REMAINS OF THE FOUNDER OF THE TEMPLE, JOSEP MARIA BOCABELLA, AND HIS FAMILY.

04. CHAPEL OF THE SACRED HEART
IMAGE OF JESUS PRESIDING OVER THE ALTAR OF THIS APSIDAL CHAPEL.

05. CHAPEL OF THE IMMACULATE CONCEPTION
LOCATED IN THE APSIDAL AREA IT HOLDS AN IMAGE OF THE VIRGIN AND ITS CORBELS ARE INSPIRED BY THE ANGELS OF THE APOCALYPSE, SUCH AS THOSE IN THE CHAPEL DEDICATED TO SAINT JOSEPH.

THE CRYPT CHAPELS

The crypt, which on the subterranean level occupies the same area as the presbytery in the upper temple, is home to 12 chapels. Seven are organised in a semi-circle, set into the apsidioles, and five others are on the straight side of this semicircular floor. The chapels in the apse are devoted to members of Jesus' family and are covered with crossed vaults whose ribs transform into columns attached to the wall and are broken up by corbels. The centre chapel, situated opposite the main altar, is dedicated to Saint Joseph, patriarch of the Catholic Church and Patron Saint of the Christian association founded by Josep Maria Bocabella, the temple's promoter. Going around it is the chapel dedicated to the Sacred Heart —which symbolizes Christ's love for Mankind—, the Immaculate Conception one —dedicated to the Virgin Mary—, Saint Joachim's and Saint Anne's chapels —Mary's parents—, her cousins' chapel —Saint Elizabeth and Saint Zachariah—, and Saint John the Baptist's chapel, son of the latter pair. The main altar takes up the central chapel on the opposite wall and it is presided over by a relief of the Holy Family, work of Catalan sculptor Josep Llimona. On the far ends of this wall are the chapels of Saint Christ, which holds the remains of Bocabella and his family, and the Virgin of Carmen one, with Antoni Gaudí's tomb.

THE ANGELS OF THE CHAPELS. THE RIBS ON THE VAULTS THAT SHAPE THE APSIDAL CHAPELS TRANSFORM INTO FOUR ATTACHED COLUMNS THAT CIRCLE APPROXIMATELY HALF OF THE WALL AND FINISH IN STRIKING CORBELS WITH SYMBOLIC AND DECORATIVE MOTIFS. IN THE SAINT JOSEPH CHAPEL, THESE COR-BELS REPRESENT TWO, FOUR AND SIX WINGED ANGELS, INSPIRED BY THE TEXTS OF THE APOCALYPSE OF SAINT JOHN. THE CHAPEL OF THE IMMACULATE CON-CEPTION ALSO BOASTS SCULPTED CORBELS OF IDENTICAL INSPIRATION.

THE KEYSTONES. THE 22 VAULTS THAT SUPPORT THE CRYPT'S ROOF ARE DECORATED WITH CARVED POLYCHROME KEYSTONES OF CIRCULAR SHAPE AND NOTABLE SIZE. THE KEYSTONES ON THE DEAMBULATORY VAULTS CONTAIN REPRESENTATIONS OF WINGED ANGELS (1), WHILE THOSE ON THE SURROUNDING CHAPELS, INCLUDING THE ONE WITH THE HIGH ALTAR, HAVE MONOGRAMS RELATING TO A SAINT OR THE MARIAN DEDICATION TO WHICH EACH ONE IS DEVOTED: SAINT JOSEPH (2), THE IMMACULATE CONCEPTION (3) AND SAINT ANNE (4), MOTHER OF THE VIRGIN MARY.

THE KEYSTONE ON THE CENTRAL VAULT

AMONGST THE 22 SCULPTED POLYCHROME KEYSTONES THAT DECORATE THE CRYPT VAULTS, THE LARGEST AND MOST ARTISTIC ONE IS THE ONE THAT TOPS THE CENTRAL VAULT, WORK OF SCULPTOR JOAN FLOTATS, WHICH REPRODUCES THE SCENE OF THE ANNUNCIATION OF THE ARCHANGEL GABRIEL TO MARY. THE RELIEF REPRESENTS THE VIRGIN KNEELING BEFORE THE ARCHANGEL WITH CROSSED ARMS SHOWING SUBMISSION AND LOYALTY. GABRIEL INFORMS HER THAT SHE HAS BEEN CHOSEN BY GOD TO CARRY JESUS, WHILE THE HOLY SPIRIT DESCENDS ON MARY IN THE SHAPE OF A DOVE AND CONSUMES THE CONCEPTION. ON THE RELIEF, GOLDEN HUES PREDOMINATE ON THE POLYCHROME WORK, AND AN INSCRIPTION IN RED CHARACTERS REPRODUCES THE FIRST WORDS OF THE 'AVE MARIA' IN LATIN. THE FINAL STRETCHES OF THE TWELVE THICK RIBS THAT TERMINATE IN THE KEYSTONE ARE DECORATED WITH POLYCHROME PAINTINGS BASED ON GEOMETRIC AND NATURALISTIC SHAPES.

01

02

01. THE VAULTS

IN ORDER NOT TO WASTE CONTRIBUTIONS MADE BY WORSHIPPERS, GAUDÍ COULDN'T MOVE TOO FAR WAY FROM THE ORIGINAL PROJECT OF THE CRYPT, WHICH HIS PREDECESSOR HAD ALREADY BEGUN. NONETHELESS, WITH THE SHAFTS OF THE PILLARS ALMOST COMPLETE, THE ARTIST DESIGNED NEW CAPITALS AND DECIDED TO RAISE THE CENTRAL VAULT ABOVE THE LEVEL OF THE REST OF THE ROOFS OF THE CRYPT, SO THAT LARGER WINDOWS COULD BE INSTALLED TO PROVIDE MORE LIGHT TO THIS UNDERGROUND FLOOR. THESE OPENINGS RECEIVE LIGHT FROM THE PRESBYTERY SITUATED JUST ABOVE.

02. STAINED GLASS

ONE OF THE BIGGEST MODIFICATIONS THAT GAUDÍ INTRODUCED IN THE CRYPT WAS TO DIG A DITCH AROUND IT TO PROVIDE LIGHT AND VENTILATION. THIS DECISION ALLOWED OPENINGS IN THE CRYPT CHAPELS. IN THE IMAGE, THE STAINED GLASS PANES OF THESE WINDOWS REPRESENT ANGELS THAT ANNOUNCE THE LAST JUDGEMENT.

THE APSE, NATURE PORTRAYED IN HONOUR OF THE VIRGIN MARY

THE LIZARD
A MULTITUDE OF REPTILES AND AMPHIBIANS RUN UP AND DOWN THE APSE FAÇADE.

...Gaudí used gargoyles that were based on real animals...

03

PERFECTION OF THE GOTHIC

In the second half of the 19th century, the worship of the Virgin underwent a period of splendour, emphasized with the anniversary, in 1880, of the Monastery of Montserrat's millenary celebrations and the subsequent proclamation of this Virgin as Patron Saint of Catalonia. Gaudí got caught up in this spiritual fervour when designing the apse's symbolic framework and dedicated all the outside wing to Mary –to whom he was very devoted–, whereas the seven interior chapels are dedicated to the Sorrows and Joys of Saint Joseph, according to the wish of Josep Maria Bocabella, the temple's promoter. Moreover, the cimborio on the apse, higher than the already finished towers, will be topped, according to Gaudí's plan, with the *Stella Matutina* (Venus), a classic Marian symbol that will crown, once the temple is finished, one of the monument's most complex areas. Started in 1891, once the crypt was finished, and completed 4 years later, the apse is the first element of the temple totally carried out by Gaudí, despite the fact that he was obliged to adhere to the configuration set out in the crypt by Francesc de Paula del Villar, his predecessor. In fact, the apse is an outward extension of the crypt's silhouette. Although its lines are clearly neo-Gothic, following the apsidal shapes planned by Del Villar for the underground level, many of its structural and decorative solutions already respond to the creative genius of Gaudí, who calls "the perfecting of the Gothic" the personal style that he applies on the rear façade of the temple. As well as persisting in his wish to erect walls with neither buttresses nor flying buttresses, constructive elements to which were scornfully referred to as "crutches for lame buildings", Gaudí exaggerates the arrises on the apse in order to generate chiaroscuros that bring out the volume of the arrangement: "Projecting elements must be combined with recess- →

es, in such a way that each convex element, placed in full light, puts the other into shadow", commented the genius on this matter. Indeed, the sun in the morning and at dusk throws light laterally on to the semi-hexagonal volumes of the chapels, leaving some stones in semi-darkness and others in light, according to their position. ❧ The pointed windows that take up practically all of the wall, and the pinnacles that crown the arrangement clearly take their inspiration from the Gothic style. However, whereas Gothic sculptors produced imaginary beings when creating gargoyles, Gaudí resorted to his great master, Nature, and produced real life creatures instead: reptiles and amphibians that fulfil three functions: decorative –they are visible from street level thanks to their large size–, constructive –they drain away water from the roofs– and symbolic: they are creatures secularly associated with evil, which are positioned head down fleeing from the purity of the symbols that top the towers dedicated to Mary and Jesus, exempt from entering inside the temple, reserved for pure souls. ❧ The pinnacles, on the other hand, form an impenetrable forest of species from the kingdom of vegetables connected to the Christian and Mediterranean world, such as wheat ears –wheat is a Eucharist symbol–, the palm tree, the olive, the fir, the cypress tree or lavender. ❧

THE APSE IN 1892
ONCE THE STRUCTURAL PART OF THE CRYPT WAS COMPLETE, WORK ON THIS PART OF THE EXPIATORY TEMPLE WAS STARTED IN 1891, AND THE PHOTOGRAPH ALONGSIDE ILLUSTRATES WHAT STAGE IT HAD REACHED AFTER JUST UNDER A YEAR OF CONSTRUCTION WORK. THE WALLS AND WINDOWS WERE ALMOST FINISHED AND WOULD EVENTUALLY BE TOPPED WITH THE PINNACLES DECORATING THE STRUCTURE THAT ARE SO ADMIRED TODAY.

01

THE VEGETABLE KINGDOM ON THE APSE

IN CONTRAST TO THE REP-
RESENTATIONS OF ANIMALS,
FACING DOWNWARDS ON
THE WALLS, THE VEGETA-
BLES CHOSEN BY GAUDÍ
–PALM LEAVES, CYPRESS,
OLIVE AND CEDAR AND
WHEAT OR LAVENDER
EARS– HAUGHTILY CROWN
THE PINNACLES ON THE
APSE. APART FROM BEING
RELIGIOUS SYMBOLS AND
POSSESSING AN UNDENIA-
BLY MEDITERRANEAN CHAR-
ACTER, GAUDÍ IS SAID TO
HAVE CHOSEN SOME OF
THESE PLANTS BECAUSE
THEY WERE ON THE SITE OF
THE TEMPLE BEFORE CON-
STRUCTION WORK COM-
MENCED.

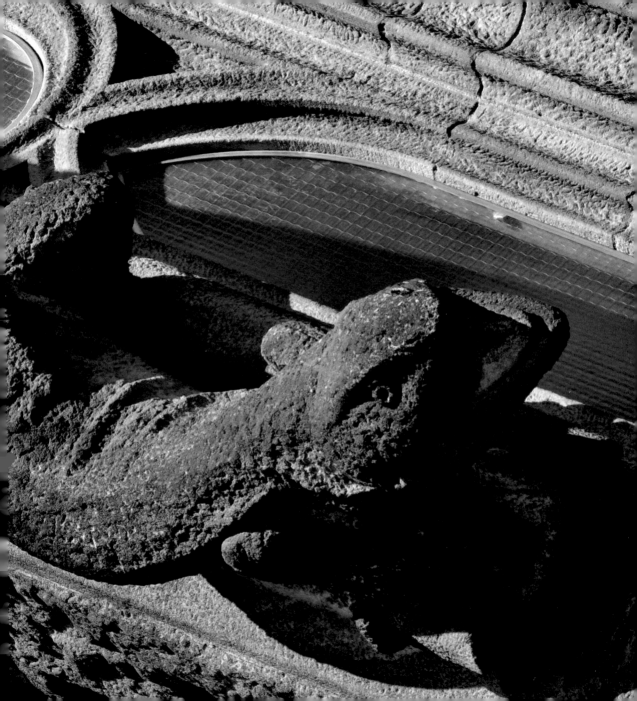

🐌 **THE APSE'S ANIMAL KINGDOM.** ON ITS NEO-GOTHIC BACKDROP, GAUDÍ ARRANGED COUNTLESS CREATURES –MANY OF WHICH ARE REPTILES AND AMPHIBIANS– THAT BREAK UP THE DISCIPLINE OF THE GEOMETRIC FORMS WITH THEIR SERPENTINE BODIES, ALWAYS POSITIONED DOWNWARDS, THEY CAN BE EASILY MADE OUT DUE TO THEIR LARGE DIMENSIONS. THERE ARE LIZARDS (1), SNAILS (2), FROGS (3), SNAKES (4) AND WALL LIZARDS (PREVIOUS DOUBLE PAGE). REPRESENTA-TIONS OF SALAMANDERS , SEA SNAILS AND CHAMELEONS CAN ALSO BE FOUND.

CONTRASTING WITH THE NATURALIST REPRESENTATIONS OF ANIMALS AND PLANTS, GAUDÍ HAD CERTAIN PARTS OF THE APSE FAÇADE DECORATED WITH SYMBOLS ASSOCIATED WITH THE HOLY FAMILY: SUCH AS THE VIRGIN'S ANAGRAM: THE CROWN OVER MARY'S INITIAL (5); SAINT JOSEPH'S SYMBOL: HIS INITIAL IS DECORATED WITH DAFFODILS, THE FLOWER THAT REPRESENTS CHASTITY (6); JESUS' SYMBOL: HIS INITIAL FRAMED BY A CROWN OF THORNS (7); AND THAT OF CHRIST: THE LETTERS ALPHA AND OMEGA; SYMBOL OF THE BEGINNING AND THE END (8).

A CLOISTER THAT SURROUNDS AND ISOLATES THE TEMPLE

THE ROSARY PORTAL
CLOSE UP OF 'THE TEMPTATION OF WOMAN',
BY SCULPTOR ETSURO SOTOO.

*...in this space
the architect
demonstrated
his great
practicality...*

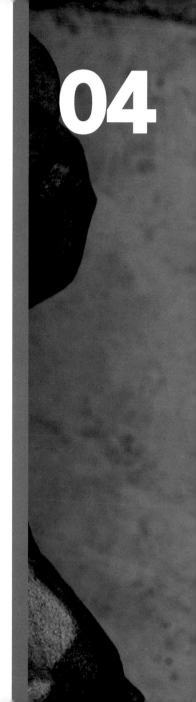

BREAKING WITH TRADITION

Sagrada Familia's cloister is a good example of how prac-
tical Gaudí was, an architect better known for his exqui-
site formal sensibility than for the solidity and originality
of his constructive contributions. When planning the
monument, Gaudí was faced with a great challenge: he
wanted to increase the temple's width to five naves, initially
planned to have only three by Francesc de Paula del Villa, his predecessor. This would mean that the distance between the two far
ends of the crossing arm would be increased by sixty metres, measurements that, concentrated on this Eixample block, would make
it rather difficult to construct a traditionally shaped cloister for Sagrada Familia. ∾ Gaudí not only rose to the challenge, but even
managed to improve the features of these architectonic spaces
that are so important to monastery and ecclesiastical life. Instead
of putting the cloister to one side, as former masters of architecture would have done in other periods, from Romanic monasteries
and Gothic cathedrals to 19th century convents, Gaudí created a
spacious walkway that went right around the temple –240 metres
in total– by means of the repetition, in the way of a gallery, of a
stretch characterized by an ornamental triangular fronton, ogival
rose windows, accompanied by windows facing outwards and with
cross vaults inside. The gallery floor is at the same height of the
temple nave, which means that the difference in floor level with
street level could be taken advantage of by constructing a mezza-
nine that functioned as warehouse, workshop or anything else. ∾
With this innovative proposal, the cloister continues to fulfil its traditional purpose but has added features: it unifies the different
sections of the monument; organizes movement from one area to
another; soundproofs the temple from street noise and allows for
processions to move around it. In order to provide continuity   →

around the circumference of the Sagrada Familia, Gaudí put doors on either side of the Nativity and Passion façades. Dedicated to different Marianist names (Rosary, Montserrat, Mercedes and Sorrows), the architect designed the first of them to demonstrate to temple workers how the decoration of the temple should be. ✎ The Rosary portal, which is situated towards the right hand side of the Nativity façade, stands out for its outstanding sculptural decoration and for the lantern that illuminates it, whose slender conical shape can be admired from the exterior. In honour to the Virgin to which it is dedicated, all of its constructive elements are decorated with roses sculpted in stone, in a work that unifies beauty and great craftsmanship. Unfortunately, the original sculptures on this portal were destroyed during the Spanish Civil War but have recently been sculpted again by Japanese sculptor Etsuro Sotoo. ✎ According to Antoni Gaudí's original project, the cloister area is completed with three independent elements: two enormous sacristies that measure thirty-five metres high, located on the angles of the apse façade, and the chapel dedicated to the Assumption, found on the axis of this same façade. In order to design this chapel, of square ground plan and which rises up thirty metres high, Gaudí was inspired by a chapel that holds the same Virgin in the Cathedral of Girona. ✎

✎
**01. SYMBOL OF
THE VIRGIN**
LOCATED ON A CLOISTER WINDOW, IT SHOWS MARY'S INITIAL AND THE DUCAL CROWN.

✎
02. THE HOLY FAMILY
THE SYMBOL THAT JOINS THE THREE MEMBERS OF THE HOLY FAMILY, SITUATED ON THE BASE OF THE LANTERN ON THE ROSARY PORTAL, IS FORMED BY JESUS' CROSS, JOSEPH'S CARPENTER'S SAW AND THE VIRGIN'S INITIAL.

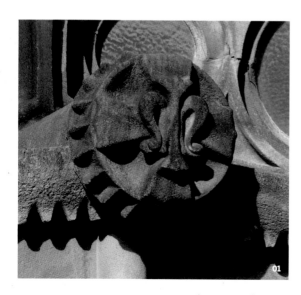

THE ROSARY DOORWAY, BEFORE THE WAR

IMAGE OF THE DOORWAY BEFORE IT WAS DESTROYED, IN 1936, DURING THE FIRST FEW DAYS OF THE SPANISH CIVIL WAR. IN FRONT OF THE DOOR A BAPTISM PILE, WHICH DISAPPEARED DURING LOOTING AND WASN'T LATER REPLACED. THE ORIGINAL ROSARY DOORWAY WAS FINISHED IN 1899 TO SERVE AS AN EXAMPLE OF HOW THE DECORATION OF THE TEMPLE SHOULD BE. IN 1982 AND 1983, SCULPTOR ETSURO SOTOO, GREAT ADMIRER OF ANTONI GAUDÍ'S WORK –HE HAS BEEN LIVING IN BARCELONA SINCE 1978 IN ORDER TO WORK ON THE TEMPLE OF THE SAGRADA FAMILIA–, HAS RESTORED THE MONUMENT SUCH AS IT CAN BE ADMIRED TODAY. AT PRESENT, ALL OF ITS WALLS, VAULTS AND ARCHES ARE DECORATED WITH NUMEROUS ROSES SCULPTED IN STONE WITH GREAT PRECISION AND DELICACY. THE TYMPANUM ON THE DOORWAY HOLDS AN IMAGE OF THE VIRGIN OF THE ROSARY, WHO IS FLANKED BY SAINTS DOMINGO AND CATALINA, WHILE ON BOTH SIDES CHARACTERS FROM THE OLD TESTAMENT ARE REPRESENTED: KING DAVID AND KING SOLOMON, AND THE PROPHETS ISAAC AND JACOB.

01. **THE ROSARY VIRGIN.** CLOSE UP OF THE IMAGE THAT PRESIDES OVER THE TYMPANUM. 02. **THE DEATH OF JUST.** THE VIRGIN, ACCOMPANIED BY JOSEPH, SHOWS THE CHILD JESUS TO A DYING MAN, WHOSE FACE IS LIKE GAUDÍ'S, IN A HOMAGE TO THE ARCHITECT. 03. **ANGEL.** SIX OF THE EIGHT CORBELS THAT SUPPORT THE COLUMNS OF THE CUPOLA, ARE DECORATED WITH DELICATE SCULPTURES OF ANGELS. 04. **THE CUPOLA.** DESPITE ITS SMALL DIMENSIONS, THE PORTAL IS EXTREMELY WELL ILLUMINATED THANKS TO ITS CUPOLA. 05. **ROSARY.** THE PORTAL'S WALLS ARE DECORATED.

WITH SCULPTED ROSARIES. **06. ROSES.** THE EXPLOSION OF ROSES THAT FLOOD ALL THE DOORWAY STEM FROM THE IMAGE OF THE ROSARY VIRGIN SITUATED ON THE TYMPANUM. **Following page 07. THE TEMPTATION OF WOMAN.** WORK OF ETSURO SOTOO, FOLLOWING THE ORIGINAL MODEL, WHICH SYMBOLIZES A DIABOLICAL MONSTER OF FISH-LIKE FORM AND TEMPTS WOMAN WITH A BAG OF MONEY. **08. THE TEMPTATION OF MAN.** SYMBOL OF VIOLENCE, A DEVIL OFFERS AN ORSINI BOMB TO A WORKER, WHICH WAS USED BY ANARCHISTS OF THE PERIOD.

THE NATIVITY FAÇADE, GAUDÍ'S LAST MASTERPIECE

JESUS CARPENTER
IN A TENDER SCENE, AN ADOLESCENT JESUS
HELPS HIS FATHER IN THE WORKSHOP.

*...the sculptures
convey the
optimism on
the Messiah's
arrival...*

PARADIGM OF THE GAUDIAN TEMPLE

A n expert on the construction process of the great medieval cathedrals, which spanned the duration of various centuries, Gaudí conveyed a combination of modesty and pragmatism when he claimed "it is not possible that just one single generation can erect an entire cathedral; we must therefore leave such a vigorous example behind, in order that following generations feel the need to continue". The rigorous example to which the architect referred was the Nativity façade, whose building work lasted thirty-eight years. In the year 1894, once the apse was completed, digging commenced in order to lay the foundations of the Nativity façade. In 1932, six years after Gaudí's death, the pinnacles on its three portals were decoratively crowned, with some sculptures still remaining to be done. Even though the architect was not able to see work completely finished before his accidental death, the Nativity façade is the only part of the temple with Antoni Gaudí's exclusive signature and which he got to see practically finished. This section –the universal example of Gaudian work in its most strictest sense– allowed him to demonstrate the detail and terminations that he so desired for the entire work. On this façade, Gaudí depicts the episodes that are related to the conception, birth, childhood and adolescence of Jesus, starting from the Annunciation up to his meeting with the priests in the temple. Sculptors were commissioned to translate the architect's project to stone while showing the more human side of the Messiah, with scenes bursting with energy, tenderness and dynamism. In line with the generic symbolism that it proposes, full of optimism, the façade is north-east facing, which means its sculptures receive the warm glow of the first light of dawn. Dominated by the four bell towers on this side, the monumental arrangement is →

made up of three porticos, a central one and two side ones, the latter ones being half the width of the former. Separated by two monumental columns attached to the façade, these three porticos, which the eastern wing of the crossing arm can be accessed by, are lodged in recesses in between the bases of the four towers and are devoted to the three members of the Holy Family, each one of them associated with a theological virtue: Mary personifies Faith, Joseph is Hope, and Jesus, in the centre, Charity. ᗫ Over this great mural area that the three porticos provide, Gaudí and his team of sculptors –with his great friend, sculptor Llorenç Matamala, at the helm– planned and made an arrangement aimed at celebrating Creation: Nature in all its splendour honours the arrival of the Messiah. In order to bring all this symbolism closer to the viewer, Antoni Gaudí included popular resources –tools from different professions along with pets and farm animals–, elements that people of the time could easily relate to. ᗫ Nonetheless, even though simplicity and humility predominate on the compositions of the façade, the artist does also include more mystical and transcendental symbols, such as the Tree of Life, which majestically tops the Charity portico –lending it a vertical dynamism that competes with the bell towers– and symbolizes the triumph of Jesus' legacy on Earth. ᗫ

ᗫ
THE BUILDING WORK ON THE NATIVITY FAÇADE
IN CONSTRUCTION SINCE 1894, THE NATIVITY FAÇADE LOOKED LIKE THIS THREE YEARS LATER, IN 1897, WITH THE PORTALS' STRUCTURE FINISHED AND SOME SCULPTURES ALREADY PUT INTO POSITION, BUT WITH NO SIGN YET OF THE BELL TOWERS THAT WERE BUILT, THIRTY FIVE YEARS LATER, MEASURING MORE THAN 100 METRES HIGH.

ᗫ
Following page
THE COLUMNS
TWO VERY HIGH PILLARS ATTACHED TO THE WALL SEPARATE THE THREE PORTICOS ON THE NATIVITY FAÇADE. AT THEIR BASE, TURTLES ARE SCULPTED, A SYMBOL OF LACK OF CHANGE OWING TO ITS LONGEVITY. THE TURTLE ON THE COLUMN NEAREST TO THE COAST IS THE TYPE BELONGING TO THE OCEAN AND THE ONE NEARER TO THE MOUNTAIN IS TERRESTRIAL. TO CONTRAST WITH PERMANENCE, GAUDÍ PUT A CHAMELEON –SYMBOL OF CHANGE– ON BOTH SIDES OF THE FAÇADE, WHILE IN THE CENTRE OF THE SHAFT, INSCRIPTIONS OF JOSEPH AND MARY INDICATE TO WHOM EACH COLUMN IS DEDICATED. HIGH UP ABOVE, THE CAPITALS, FORMED BY PALM LEAVES, SUPPORT PAIRS OF TRUMPETING ANGELS THAT ARE ENTHUSIASTICALLY ANNOUNCING THE BIRTH OF THE MESSIAH.

THE ADORATION OF THE MESSIAH. SITUATED ON A LOWER PLAN AND WITH ALL EYES ON THE IMAGE OF NEWLY BORN JESUS, THE GROUPS OF THE THREE WISE MEN (1) AND THE SHEPHERDS (2) MAKE UP A CHAPTER WITH THE ARRANGEMENT OF THE HOLY FAMILY (LEFT) –SITUATED ON THE PORTAL MULLION– AND WITH THE CHANTING ANGELS AND MUSICIANS STRAIGHT AFTER ON THE NEXT LEVEL UP. SAINT JOSEPH'S STANCE CONFERS GREAT DYNAMISM TO THIS ARRANGEMENT, CARVED BY CATALAN NOVECENTISTA JAUME BUSQUETS.

Previous page

THE ANGEL MUSICIANS
SITUATED TO THE LEFT AND
RIGHT HAND SIDE OF THE
CHANTING CHERUBS, THE
ANGEL MUSICIANS PLAY
CLASSICAL INSTRUMENTS
SUCH AS THE BASSOON,
VIOLIN AND HARP, AND POP-
ULAR ONES SUCH AS THE
ZITHER, DRUM AND DULZAI-
NA. THE LATTER INSTRU-
MENTS SYMBOLIZE THE
PRESENCE OF THE PEOPLE
IN THE TEMPLE.

01. BIRDS
FLOCKS OF DUCKS AND
OTHER BIRDS GIVE LIFE AND
DYNAMISM TO THE STONE
FAÇADE.

**02. THE CORONATION
OF THE VIRGIN**
SITUATED BELOW THE
VAULTED PARABOLIC
NICHE ON THE CHARITY
PORTICO, THIS SCULPTURAL
GROUP CARVED BY JOAN
MATAMALA REPRESENTS
JESUS CROWNING THE
VIRGIN MARY FOR HER
LOVE OF GOD.

01

THE HOPE PORTICO

On a smaller scale to that of the Charity portico, still preserving some marked vertical proportions, the Hope portico –situated on the left of the Nativity façade– is dedicated to Saint Joseph and presents various sculptural groups set in a context of aquatic flora and fauna. It refers to the River Nile, given that one of the scenes represented is the Holy Family's Flight to Egypt following the appearance of an angel in one of Joseph's dreams warning of the Slaughter of the Innocents, a biblical fact represented in the sculptural arrangement alongside. ❧ The tympanum on the doorway is taken up with a scene of great tenderness: Jesus shows his father an injured dove while Joachim and Anna, his grandparents, look on touched by the scene. Higher up, located inside a niche covered by a catenary arch of typical Gaudí style, the architect put the episode of the betrothal of Mary and Joseph, who are blessed by a priest. ❧ On the higher section, below a pinnacle inspired by the rocky crags of the mountain of Montserrat in Catalonia, appears Saint Joseph at the helm of a boat, symbol of the Catholic Church, whose helmsman is the patriarch of the Holy Family. The similarity to Gaudí's physical appearance is an apparent homage made by the workers of the temple to the architect after his death in 1926. ❧

❧
01. JOSEPH'S BOAT
LOCATED HIGH UP ON THE HOPE PORTICO, BELOW THE SHAPES THAT EMULATE MONTSERRAT'S ROCKY CRAGS, THIS GROUP SHOWS THE PATRIARCH OF THE CHURCH WITH A PHYSICAL LIKENESS TO GAUDÍ. IT IS SAID TO BE A HOMAGE TO THE ARTIST ON BEHALF OF THE TEMPLE'S WORKERS.

❧
02. THE FLIGHT TO EGYPT
AN ANGEL GUIDES THE HOLY FAMILY SAFELY ON TO EGYPT SO THAT JESUS DOESN'T FALL PREY TO HEROD'S SLAUGHTER OF THE INNOCENTS.

❧
03. THE DRAGONFLY
THE FLORA AND FAUNA OF THE NILE ARE REPRESENTED ALL OVER THE PORTAL.

01. THE ROSARY

OVER THE SMALL ROSE WINDOW OF THE HOPE PORTICO HANG VARIOUS ROSARY BEADS EACH WITH SEVEN ROWS OF SEVEN BEADS. THESE ARE ROSARIES OF THE SEVEN SORROWS OF THE VIRGIN MARY.

02. TOOLS

THE LINTEL ON THE PORTICO IS PACKED WITH REPRESENTATIONS OF CARPENTRY TOOLS, IN HONOUR OF SAINT JOSEPH, THE CARPENTER.

03. FARM ANIMALS

THE GEESE AND DUCKS THAT APPEAR ON THE PORTICO REFER TO THE FLUVIAL FAUNA OF THE NILE, IN REFERENCE TO THE HOLY FAMILY'S FLIGHT TO EGYPT, AND ARE ALSO THERE TO CAPTURE THE ATTENTION OF THE HUMBLE FAMILIES WHO WORK ON THE LAND.

04. THE DEATH OF THE INNOCENT SAINTS

A CALLOUS SOLDIER GETS READY TO KILL A NEWLY BORN, CRUELLY IGNORING THE DESPERATE PLEAS OF ITS MOTHER, IN A DRAMATIC SCENE THAT GREATLY CONTRASTS WITH THE GENERAL JOY THAT IS TRANSMITTED BY THE NATIVITY FAÇADE.

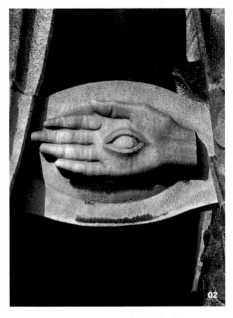

02

03

THE FAITH PORTICO

Situated on the right of the Nativity façade, the Faith portico is dedicated to the Virgin as maximum exponent of this theological virtue, though the protagonist of most of the scenes is the infant and adolescent Jesus: he is seen in the arms of the priest Simon, working in Saint Joseph's workshop and preaching in the temple, before the surprise and admiration of his parents. ୬ In homage to the Virgin, Gaudí had the Visitation to Elizabeth sculpted and, high up on the portal –below the wheat ears and the grapes that represent the Eucharist–, the Immaculate Conception, which appears over a three-point lamp, symbol of the Holy Trinity. ୬ In order to obtain natural poses, Gaudí studied the human anatomy in great detail and also borrowed a skeleton from a hospital which he used to aid him find the best postures, then reproduced them later on a model, which he would photograph surrounded by mirrors, in order to control the different angles of vision of the future sculpture. Once the posture was chosen, the model was covered with material soaked with plaster in order to create a mould. Once the figure's location on the façade was decided, Gaudí would continue to correct its size, increasing the height of the sculptures placed higher up, in order that they would be seen with the same scale as those situated nearer the observer. ୬

01. JESUS IN SIMON'S ARMS

WHEN JOSEPH AND MARY INTRODUCE THEIR SON TO THE TEMPLE, AS HEBREW LAW DICTATES, SIMON AND ANNA PREDICT THAT JESUS WILL BE THE MESSIAH AND BLESS HIM.

02. THE VISITATION

MARY REUNITES WITH HER COUSIN ELIZABETH IN ORDER TO INFORM HER THAT SHE WILL GIVE BIRTH TO THE MESSIAH.

03. THE IMMACULATE CONCEPTION

THE FIGURE OF THE VIRGIN WITH HER ARMS CROSSED ON HER CHEST RECALL THIS DOGMA OF THE CATHOLIC CHURCH.

04. JESUS PREACHES IN THE TEMPLE

THE CENTRAL SCENE ON THE FAITH PORTICO, OVER THE DOOR LINTEL, SHOWS THE MESSIAH, AT JUST 12 YEARS OF AGE, EXPLAINING TO THE DOCTORS THE PRE-CISE MEANING OF THE HOLY SCRIPTURES.

THE TREE OF LIFE

The simplicity of the biblical motifs chosen for the sculptural decoration on the façade, most of it being very popular due to its connection to Christmas or the more human side of Jesus' life, contrasts with the symbolic depth of the very high pinnacle that seems to compete with the bell towers and tops the Charity portico and the Nativity façade arrangement. Antoni Gaudí, in fact, reserved this space in order to represent the Tree of Life, a symbolic compendium of the three porticos and allegory of Jesus' legacy: the promise of eternal life. The tree is a cypress, which is a symbol of eternal life due to the perennial nature of its leaves and its hard-wearing wood. Its rich green shades contrast with and stand out from the grey stone, hinting at the effect that the polychrome technique would have had if it had been used on all temple sculptures and structures as outlined by Gaudí. ✍

In order to crown the cypress tree, the architect used the sign of the Holy Trinity, while the grand total of twenty-one doves flutter around the tree. The original ones were made in alabaster work, but the majority were replaced later on with marble ones in the year 1990. At the foot of the cypress tree, a pelican –symbol of the Eucharist– feeds its hungry offspring and is situated between two stairs that symbolize the aspiration of obtaining the everlasting life. ✍

✍
01. THE CYPRESS
SURROUNDED BY DOVES, THE TREE OF LIFE IS ONE OF THE FEW POLYCHROME ELEMENTS ON THE ENTIRE FACADE.

✍
02 AND 03. ANGELS WITH BREAD AND WINE
ONE COLLECTS CHRIST'S BLOOD AND THE OTHER HIS BODY, METAPHOR FOR THE EUCHARIST.

✍
04. ANGEL CARRYING INCENSE
VARIOUS ANGELS SCATTER HOLY SMOKE WITH THEIR CENSERS, AS A SIGN OF PURIFICATION.

✍
05. THE HOLY TRINITY
THE 'T' OF 'THEOS' (GOD IN GREEK) AND THE 'X' OF CHRIST, CROWNED BY THE DOVE SYMBOL OF THE HOLY SPIRIT, CROWNS THE TOP OF THE TREE OF LIFE.

✍
06. THE PELICAN
IN THE PAST IT WAS BELIEVED THAT THIS BIRD OPENED ITS CHEST TO FEED ITS OFFSPRING, FOR WHICH IT WAS TRANSFORMED INTO A EUCHARIST SYMBOL.

✍
07. JESUS' ANAGRAM
THE LATIN INITIALS, JHS, WHICH STAND FOR JESUS, SAVIOUR OF MANKIND, FRAMED BY THE CROSS OF SACRIFICE, ON WHOSE SIDES GAUDÍ HAD THE LETTER ALPHA AND OMEGA ENGRAVED, THE FIRST AND FINAL LETTERS OF THE GREEK ALPHABET WHICH SYMBOLIZE THE BEGINNING AND THE END.

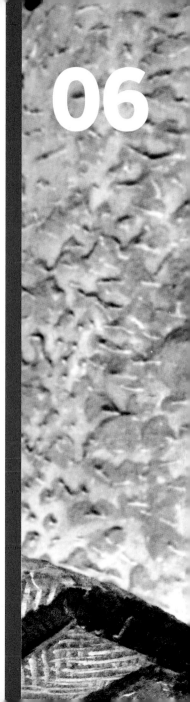

THE PASSION FAÇADE, JESUS' PAIN IN STONE AND BRONZE

06

PONTIUS PILATE
REPRESENTATION OF ROMAN PREFECT PONTIUS PILATE IN SCULPTURAL GROUP 'ECCE HOMO'.

...Gaudí contrived this façade to be cold and austere...

THE REPRESENTATION OF DEATH

In the year 1911, Gaudí became ill with Maltese fever and decided to move to the Pyrenean municipality of Puigcerdà in order to recuperate in a healthier climate and escape polluted, industrial Barcelona. In this unavoidable retirement, the artist comes so near to death that he even decides to draw up a will. These weeks of pain and suffering inspire him to design the Passion façade, which on the south-west side of the temple relates the final days of Jesus on Earth. When designing the general project of the Temple of the Sagrada Família, Gaudí decided to dedicate its three façades –the fourth one is taken up by the apse– to the most transcendental moments of Jesus' life: the Birth, Passion and Resurrection. In order to generate a wave of optimism in the city as regards the construction of the temple, the architect decided that the Nativity façade, the most joyous and festive, should be the first one constructed. At that time, at the beginning of the 1890's, Gaudí already planned on giving the Passion façade a dark air, and believed that starting to show his iconographic project for Sagrada Familia on this side might result being counterproductive for the development of the work. "There might be those who find this façade as too extravagant, but I wanted it to frighten, and on trying to do so will not cut back on chiaroscuro", explained Gaudí when discussing with collaborators the project for this portico, which is facing the west, sunset, in a location that reinforces its lugubrious symbolic load. Indeed, the architect's sketches convey the entire bleakness and agony of the Passion. The artist conceived the architecture and sculpture on this façade with premeditated coldness and austerity, in sharp contrast to the warmth and vitality exuded by the Nativity façade. There is no decoration. Its walls are naked contours, with the viewer's gaze focusing in on the twelve sculptural →

groups that chronologically describe the final days of Christ before his Resurrection. ❧ In front of the wall, six leaning columns increase the general sensation of nudity with the harshness of their forms. The base, the shaft and capital of these columns follow one another without any ornamental interruption, with wide grooves that stretch the length of their entire height, creating enormous stone sequoia trees that support the angular roof on which Gaudí projected an original frontage supported by eighteen narrow pillars of bone-like appearance. ❧ Fortunately, the architect's sketches survived the fire in his workshop during the Spanish Civil War and in 1954 –after a number of years restoring documents, plans and models– served as inspiration in order that construction work on the temple and on this façade would be resumed once again. ❧ The portico structure complete and the façade's four bell towers' crowned, Catalan sculptor Josep Maria Subirachs was to accept the challenging commission in 1986 to depict in stone and bronze the pain and sadness that Antoni Gaudí had envisaged for this monumental façade. The personal contribution of Subirachs, who applied very similar working methods to those used by Antoni Gaudí in his latter years, led to the first large element of the temple being carried out after the death of its great maker. ❧

01

THE ICONOGRAPHIC PROJECT

THE PASSION FAÇADE RELATES THE MOST TRANSCENDENTAL MOMENTS OF JESUS CHRIST'S FINAL HOURS AS A GROWN MAN, CHRONOLOGICALLY ORDERED IN TWELVE SCULPTURAL ARRANGEMENTS THAT ARE A FREE INTERPRETATION OF THE TRADITIONAL ROAD TO CALVARY. SUBIRACHS DECIDED TO ORGANIZE THE SCENES INTO THREE LEVELS, IN SUCH A WAY THAT THE VIEWING ORDER FOLLOWS THE SINUOUS 'S' SHAPE, STARTING BELOW ON THE LEFT WITH THE LAST SUPPER AND FINISHING HIGH UP ON THE RIGHT WITH THE BURIAL OF CHRIST, THE LAST STAGE OF THE ROAD TO CALVARY BEFORE THE RESURRECTION. THIS ORGANIZATION LEADS TO JESUS BEING CRUCIFIED IN THE UPPER CENTRAL SPACE OF THE PORTICO, THE PRIVILEGED AREA WHERE THE VIEWER'S GAZE COMES TO REST.

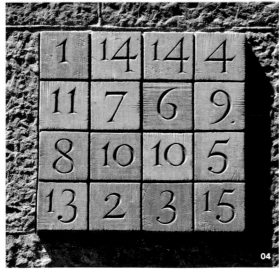

01. THE LAST SUPPER. LOCATED ON THE LEFT LOWER FAR END OF THE FAÇADE, IT IS THE FIRST BIBLICAL FACT THAT IS NARRATED. **02. JUDAS' KISS.** JESUS, COLD AND DISTANT, IS KISSED BY THE APOSTLE THAT BETRAYED HIM. **03. THE SERPENT.** DETAIL OF THE SCULPTURAL GROUP FROM THE KISS OF JUDAS, THE SNAKE REPRESENTS THE DEVIL. **04. THE CRYPTOGRAM.** IT CONTAINS 16 NUMBERS WHOSE SUM, IN 310 DIFFERENT COMBINATIONS, ALWAYS COME TO 33, WHICH WAS CHRIST'S AGE WHEN HE DIED. **05. THE SECRET DISCUSSION.** IN HIS SKETCHES, GAUDÍ SET OUT TWO OF THESE SECRET MEETING PLACES, ONE PLACED ON EACH SIDE OF THE FAÇADE.

THE FLAGELLATION OF CHRIST

Sculptor Josep Maria Subirachs decided to give special importance to one of the parts of the Road to Calvary –the Flagellation of Christ– dedicating a free-standing sculptural arrangement in a preferential location, in front of the door mullion, at the same level that people leave and enter the temple. Carved in travertine marble, the flagellation shows Jesus alone and beaten, tied to a column, after being tortured by the soldiers. Subirachs put this group in the centre of the façade, forming a narrative unit with the crucifixion –high up on the portal– and the Ascension –on the walkway in between the two central towers–. The three steps on which the column is set symbolize the three days that passed between the crucifixion of Jesus Christ and the Resurrection.

SUBIRACHS, THE SCULPTOR

After accepting the commission to carry out the sculptures on the Passion façade, Subirachs dedicated an entire year to the study of Gaudí's work and moved into the latter's workshop inside the temple –just like the architect had–, to work exclusively on this project. His angular and schematic carving are very much in keeping with the sadness that Gaudí wanted to convey and contrasts, for its abstract nature, with the figurativeness of the opposite entrance.

01. JESUS
THE FACE AND POSTURE OF THE MESSIAH REFLECT ALL THE PAIN, LONELINESS AND DESPAIR AFTER THE TORTURE OF THE FLAGELLATION.

02. THE SCULPTOR
JOSEP MARIA SUBIRACHS, IN HIS WORKSHOP IN SAGRADA FAMILIA, MODELLING THE ASCENSION OF CHRIST IN CLAY, WHICH WAS LATER CARVED IN TRAVERTINE MARBLE.

03. THE KNOT
SCULPTED WITH GREAT REALISM, IT SYMBOLIZES THE PHYSICAL TORTURE THAT JESUS CHRIST UNDERWENT.

04. THE FLAGELLATION
MEASURING FIVE METRES HIGH, DUE TO ITS DRAMATIC WEIGHT THIS ARRANGEMENT ASTOUNDS ALL THOSE WHO LEAVE AND ENTER THE TEMPLE. THE FOUR TAMBOURS OF THE COLUMN SYMBOLIZE THE ARMS OF THE CROSS. ON ONE OF THE STEPS, SUBIRACHS REPRODUCED THE CANE THAT THE SOLDIERS USED TO STRIKE JESUS INSTEAD OF THE SCEPTRE, SYMBOL OF ROYALTY. WITH THIS OBJECT, THE SCULPTOR SYMBOLIZES PHYSICAL TORTURE.

02

01

03

04

01. **ECCE HOMO.** PILATE, SITTING AND SADDENED, PRESENTS JESUS TO THE JEWS. **02. THE DENIAL OF PETER.** PETER, WRAPPED IN A SHEET, DENIES KNOWLEDGE OF JESUS. **03. ROMAN EAGLE.** IT IS SITUATED ON A COLUMN WITH THE INSCRIPTION "TIBERIUS, EMPEROR OF ROME". **04. THE COCKEREL..** CLOSE UP OF THE GROUP OF THE DENIAL, WHEN THE COCKEREL CROWS, PETER REMEMBERS JESUS' WORDS, ANTICIPATING THAT HE WOULD DENY HIS ACQUAINTANCE. **05. THE LABYRINTH.** SYMBOL RECUPERATED FROM GOTHIC CATHEDRALS, IT REPRESENTS JESUS' PATH ON BEING CAPTURED.

OSTRALLEIEN
TRES NO ENS
NGUI LLAVORS
RI FEU CRIDAR
EL DLS JUEUS?
TU AIXO O BE
LA TREPLICA
SON EL TEU
GTS EIS QUI
ANS QUE HAS
EVA REI A LESA
OS ELS MEUS
VE IO NO FOS

AN OMEN A
EL CRUCIFICAREN PI
FEU POSAR A LA CREU

JESUS Ð NATZARE

HIS SOLDATS QUAN H
JESUS VAN AGAFA
EN FEREN QUATRE
CADA SOLDAT A TA ME
TUNICA. ES DIGUERE
SORTEGEM LA A S
EL QUE DIU L'ESCRIPT
ENTRE ELLS ELS ME
JUGAT LA MEVA...R

01

03

05

SANT JORDI

LA FESTA DELS ÀZIMS

TAMBORES S'ACOSTA TOTS
VAREM HUER A PILAT
I EL ENGUIEREN
A PILAT
A CRUSIFICO

02

THE FAÇADE DOORS

Josep Maria Subirachs also sculpted the three doors on the Passion façade. In contrast to Antoni Gaudí's taste for carpentry, the sculptor decided to produce them in bronze, a material that allowed him to play with textures and inlaid work. The Gospel Doors take up the central area of the portico. Located behind the Flagellation of Christ, they are divided into two doors measuring almost six metres high that explain in words –in the Catalan language– what the sculptural groups on the façade relate in stone: texts from the Gospel concerning the last days of Jesus. This way, the two doors convert into the pages of a monumental New Testament. On the left hand side is the Door of Gethsemane, which illustrates by means of relief the prayers made by Jesus in the Garden of Gethsemane along with the sleeping disciples and biblical verses connected to this scene. On the right hand side of the arrangement, the Coronation of Thorns door holds a higher relief that represents the humiliation that the soldiers inflicted on Jesus Christ by giving him a crown of thorns after torturing him. In the central strip is, with a play of symmetries, the presentation of Jesus before Herod and Pilate, images that are accompanied by texts from Dante's Divine Comedy and verses from Catalan poet Salvador Espriu.

01. THE CRUCIFIXION AND THE VERONICA
THESE TWO GROUPS TAKE UP THE CENTRE OF THE FAÇADE, OVER THE GOSPEL DOORS.

02. JESUS FALLEN
DETAIL OF THE GROUP OF THE THREE MARYS, WHERE JESUS IS SEEN LOADED DOWN BY THE CROSS.

03. THE BURIAL
IT TAKES UP THE UPPER FAR RIGHT HAND SIDE OF THE FAÇADE AND CHRONOLOGI-CALLY IS THE LAST SCENE OF THE PASSION.

04. LONGINUS
HE WAS THE SOLDIER WHO WIELDED HIS LANCE ACROSS JESUS' SIDE ON THE CROSS. AFTERWARDS HE CONVERTED TO CHRISTIANI-TY AND DIED AS A MARTYR.

05. SOLDIERS PLAYING
SCENE IN WHICH THE SOL-DIERS PLAY WITH DICE FOR JESUS' ROBES.

Following page
THE VERONICA AND THE EVANGELIST
REPRESENTATION OF JESUS' SECOND FALTER ON THE ROAD TO CALVARY. IT IS THE MOST NUMEROUS SCULP-TURAL ARRANGEMENT ON THE PASSION FAÇADE WITH SEVENTEEN FIGURES. IN THE MIDDLE IS THE VERONICA SHOWING THE MATERIAL ON WHICH JESUS' FACE IS MARKED. SUBIRACHS ALSO DEPICTS JOHN THE BAPTIST, TO THE LEFT HAND SIDE, BUT USES ANTONI GAUDÍ'S FACE.

THE CRUCIFIXION

IT IS THE CROWNING SCULPTURAL ARRANGEMENT OF THE FAÇADE AND ITS COMPOSITION IS DELIBERATELY ASYMMETRIC, IN ORDER TO UNDERLINE THE DRAMA OF THE SCENE. MARY MAGDALENE, KNEELING, AND THE VIRGIN, COMFORTED BY SAINT JOHN, ARE PUT TO THE LEFT HAND SIDE OF CHRIST. THE CROSS IS MADE OF TWO IRON BEAMS. THE PROFILE OF THE FRONT BEAM IS HIGHLIGHTED WITH THE COLOUR RED IN ORDER TO MARK THE FIRST LETTER OF 'INRI', THE INITIALS OF "JESUS FROM NAZARETH, KING OF THE JEWS". AT THE FOOT OF THE CROSS, A SKULL SYMBOLISES DEATH, WHILE, TO THE RIGHT, THE MOON REPRESENTS THE DARKNESS OF NIGHT.

01. THE ASCENSION OF CHRIST
THE BRIDGE BETWEEN THE TWO CENTRAL BELL TOWERS OF THE PASSION FAÇADE SUPPORT A BRONZE SCULPTURE OF CHRIST IN ASCENSION. IT IS FIVE METRES HIGH AND WEIGHS TWO TONNES.

02. THE LAMB
LOCATED ON THE ATRIUM AND MADE OF LIVELY CERAMIC WORK, IT SYMBOLISES CHRIST'S RESURRECTION.

03. THE HOLY SPIRIT
A DOVE IN FLIGHT REPRE-SENTS THE THIRD PERSON IN THE HOLY TRINITY.

04. DEATH
A SKULL AT THE FOOT OF THE CROSS SYMBOLISES JESUS' DEATH AND THE PLACE WHERE HE DIED, CALLED CALVARY OR GOLGOTHA, PLACE OF THE SKULL. THE SCULPTED PIECE MEASURES AROUND A METRE.

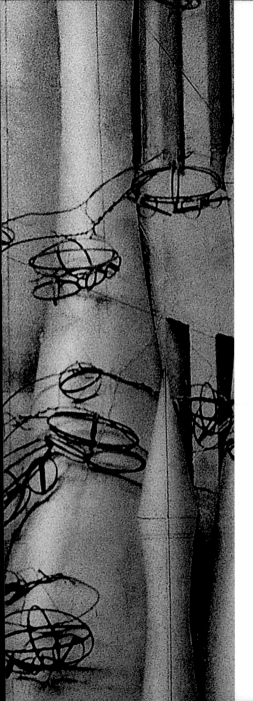

THE GLORY FAÇADE, A MONUMENTAL CATECHISM

GAUDÍ'S MODEL
LANTERN CLOSE-UP. THE MOST SIGNIFICANT CONSTRUCTIVE ELEMENT ON THE FAÇADE.

...Gaudí gave the temple's main façade a heavy symbolic load...

LEFT
RAMON BERENGUER'S
ILLUSTRATION SHOWS
THE GREAT CONSTRUC-
TIVE CHALLENGE OF THE
GLORY FAÇADE: ITS 16
LANTERNS FLANKED BY
THE BAPTISTERY CUPO-
LAS, TO THE LEFT, AND
THE PENITENCE CHAPEL
TO THE RIGHT, AND THE
ORIGINAL CLOUD ROOFS
WITH WORDS FROM THE
CREED.

BELOW
CLOSE-UP OF THE MONU-
MENT TO FIRE, WHICH
WILL BE LOCATED HIGH UP
ON THE ENTRANCE STEPS
TO THE TEMPLE OF THE
MAIN FAÇADE.

THE RESURRECTION AND LAST JUDGEMENT

As it was going to be the main entrance to the temple, Gaudí gave the Glory façade much larger dimensions than those of the façades on the crossing arm. It is planned to be one and a half times wider than the others and its four bell towers will soar higher than those on the transept. This façade is planned to be accessed by means of flights of steps situated on the site opposite and from a square constructed above Mallorca Street, result of extending outwardly the ground level of the temple. ❧ Although he didn't get round to explaining in complete detail all the constructive and symbolic elements of this façade, Gaudí left behind a model with the basic formal project and an iconographic plan that details the complex symbolism that he wanted to give this vast space. After dedicating two façades to the life of Jesus, the architect proposes devoting the main entrance of the temple to illustrate the situation of Man within the order of Creation and the paths the Gospel suggests in order to obtain happiness and Glory, converting this great area into an enormous catechism. ❧ Facing southwest, the façade enjoys the best location of the temple site, as it receives many hours of sunlight for most of the day. Its most striking constructive elements are the sixteen monumental lanterns whose height increases from the far sides to the centre. And in front of them, one of the most daring ideas in Gaudí's career: various clouds with texts of the Creed written on them. ❧ The central lantern stands out for its magnitude –it has to reach the height of the bell towers– and it is crowned by the image of God, inscribed in the triangle symbol. Lower down, Jesus judges Man and if he should go to Glory (Heaven) or Hell. And behind this scene, the slenderness of the lantern means that the rose window on the central nave can be admired, whose image of the Holy Ghost com- →

pletes the representation of the Trinity. It is planned that the arrangement of towers and lanterns is supported on eight columns that symbolize the eight Beatitudes. On this portico behind these columns the representation of the virtues, the capital sins, the gifts from the Holy Ghost, the works of mercy, manual trades, the Virgin Mary, the Saints and Saint Joseph are planned. ∽ To provide access to the interior, Gaudí proposes seven doors devoted to the sacraments and to the Lord's Prayer. The doors on the far ends are dedicated to Baptism and Penitence, given that they allow access to the Penitence Chapel, buildings of circular ground plan situated on the corners of the temple. The central door of the portico, which is bronze, is dedicated to the Eucharist and it was carried out by the sculptor Subirachs. It contains the complete text of the Lord's Prayer and the request "Lord, give us this day our daily bread", drawn from this prayer, in 50 languages. The mural area between these doors and the vaults of the portico is predicted to represent the foreseen symbolism with the history of Christianity from Adam and Eve, Purgatory as transition between Earth and Heaven, and three biblical references: Noah's Ark as a symbol of Hope; the Ark of the Covenant, in representation of the Faith, and the Holy House of Nazareth, which symbolizes Charity. ∽

∽

01. THE MAIN DOORWAY OF THE FAÇADE
WORK OF CATALAN SCULPTOR JOSEP MARIA SUBIRACHS, THE MAIN ENTRANCEWAY TO THE TEMPLE IS MADE OF BRONZE AND MEASURES FIVE METRES HIGH. ON ITS SURFACE THE WORDS FROM THE LORD'S PRAYER ARE SCULPTED IN FIFTY DIFFERENT LANGUAGES.

∽

02. ORIGINAL MODEL OF THE FAÇADE
THE MAIN VESTIGE OF ANTONI GAUDÍ'S IDEAS CONCERNING THE GLORY FAÇADE IS THIS MODEL IN WHICH HE SUGGESTS THE BASE OF THE FOUR BELL TOWERS, THE SHAPE OF THE 16 LANTERNS AND THE IMAGINATIVE CLOUDS WITH THE FIRST WORDS OF THE CREED.

02

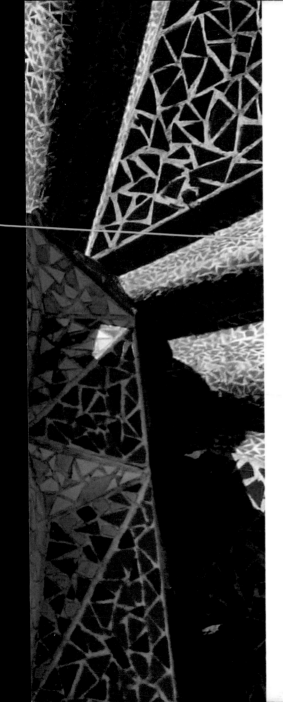

THE TOWERS, A HUMAN WORK THAT REACHES OUT TO DIVINE CREATION

08

THE BELL TOWER PINNACLES
EPISCOPAL ATTRIBUTES –MITRE, CROSS, RING
AND STAFF–CROWN THE DECORATIVE ENDINGS.

*..the cimborios
and bell towers
connect the
terrestrial with
the celestial...*

RECUPERATING GOTHIC SPIRIT

With the invention of the ogival arch and the crossed vault, the architects of the Late Middle Ages were able to construct much higher buildings with significantly lighter buttresses and walls. Due to these technical advances, prospering cities of the time competed to build cathedrals whose pinnacles soared higher and higher and nearer to heaven. Centuries later, imbued with the same spirit that had captured Gothic archi-tects, Antoni Gaudí aimed to convert Sagrada Familia into the highest construction in Barcelona. He designed the tower dedi-cated to Jesus, the temple's highest tower, to soar 170 metres high, a height that would make it the tallest religious building in the world but slightly lower than Montjuïc mountain, which was the highest hill in the municipality of Barcelona at the end of the 19th century, when Sagrada Familia's foundations were laid. With this decision, Gaudí set out with great determination to erect a building that would stand out in the city while at the same time pay humble respect to God's work –Montjuïc–, which he believed Man should not try to outdo. ⟶ The architect designed a total of 18 towers –12 bell towers and six cimborios– and only got to see one of them finished, the Barnabus tower, completed in the year 1925, a few months before he died. The remaining towers of the Nativity façade were completed in 1930 and the four on the oppo-site side, in 1978. In order to get the most visually and symbolical-ly from the great height of these constructive elements, all of the towers are topped with pinnacles decorated with glazed Venetian mosaic work whose glossy shine can be seen from a long way away. Owing to their great height, Gaudí designed the six cimbo-rios with a wider base than the bell towers and with a profile simi-lar to the sacristy ones –an octagonal base whose sides ascend in →

concave parabolas–, though with much larger dimensions than these.

⤫ The architect paid a lot of importance to the cimborios, considering them as the exaltation of the temple, given that they illuminate the altar and give the building its pyramidal shape. The larger of them, the Jesus tower, has an enormous vault which covers the intersection between the nave and the crossing arm and is topped with a 15 metre high four-armed cross, with a look-out point reached by elevator and powerful lights which highlight its silhouette at night. Flanking the Jesus tower on its four angles, Gaudí put the cimborios of the Evangelists, whose symbolic icons (the eagle for Saint John, the li-on for Saint Mark, the angel for Saint Matthew and the ox for Saint Luke) will top the pinnacles at 125 metres high. The architect also had the idea of installing two powerful light beams in each one of them, one directed at the street, symbolizing the light of the Gospel illuminating the world, and the other towards Jesus' tower, which is the temple's culminating point. ⤫ To the northeast of the temple, topping the apse area, Gaudí put the sixth cimborio of the arrangement, Mary's tower, crowned at 120 metres with the *Stella Matutina* (Venus, the morning star), a Marianist symbol whose presence preluded the dawn in the same way that the Virgin preced-ed the birth of Jesus. ⤫

THE TOWERS AND CITY

THE BELL TOWERS OF
SAGRADA FAMILIA HAVE
CONVERTED INTO THE
MOST CHARACTERISTIC
FEATURE OF THE TEMPLE
AND SYMBOL OF THE CITY
OF BARCELONA, GIVEN
THAT THEIR EXCEPTIONAL
PARABOLIC SILHOUETTE,
DECORATED WITH GLOSSY
POLYCHROME PINNACLES,
IS VISIBLE FROM ANY ELE-
VATED POINT IN THE CITY.
THE DIZZYING EFFECT
CAUSED BY THE ONE HUN-
DRED METRE HEIGHT
REACHED BY THE EIGHT
CONSTRUCTED TOWERS
ENABLES ONE TO IMAGINE
THE MONUMENTAL PRES-
ENCE OF THE CIMBORIO
DEDICATED TO JESUS, THE
HIGHEST IN THE ARRANGE-
MENT, WHICH WILL SOAR A
MAJESTIC 170 METRES
HIGH.

01. BALCONY
THIS SMALL LOOK-OUT POINT MARKS THE POINT IN THE BELL TOWER WHERE THE SQUARE SHAPED BASE BECOMES CIRCULAR.

02. THE INSCRIPTIONS
ON ONE OF THE ANGLES OF THE LOWER ZONE OF THE BELL TOWERS ARE SCULPTED THE NAMES OF THE HOLY FAMILY (JESUS, MARY, JOSEPH) BELOW PALM LEAVES, SYMBOL OF EASTER.

03. STARRED PINNACLES
THE NICHES THAT HOLD THE IMAGES OF THE APOSTLES ON THE NATIVITY FAÇADE, SUCH AS THE TOWER DEDICATED TO SIMON OF CANÁ, ARE TOPPED WITH STARS.

04. SOUND STUDIES
GAUDÍ MADE THE VENTS TILT SLIGHTLY, IN ORDER THAT THE BELLS COULD BE HEARD THROUGHOUT THE CITY.

Following page
THE APOSTLES
ON THE NATIVITY FAÇADE ARE THE IMAGES OF BARNABUS (1), MATTHIAS (2), SIMON OF CANÁ (3) AND JUDAS THADDAEUS (4). ON THE PASSION, THE APOSTLES REPRESENTED ARE THOMAS (5), JAMES THE LESSER (6), PHILIP (7) AND BARTHOLOMEW (8).

THE BELL TOWERS

Devoted to Jesus' twelve apostles, the bell towers start off with a square base and then approximately a quarter of the way up undergo an original change typical of the ingenious Gaudí, adopting a circular section which gives them their characteristic parabolic profile, possibly inspired by *Castells* –human towers traditional in Catalonia, especially in Camp de Tarragona, where Gaudí is originally from–, though their shape also reminds of north African mosques constructed with sun-dried brick or the geographical formations of Capadocia, in Turkey. The architect took advantage of this change of section from square to circular form by using the resulting arrises for the sculpture of the apostle to whom each tower is dedicated. Symbolism, however, tends to be more concentrated on the pinnacles, covered with mosaic work and crowned with the initial of the apostle to whom the bell tower is dedicated and with icons such as a mitre, cross, staff and ring– that represent the bishops' power, who continue on with the apostles' labour. Inside the bell towers, all is arranged to achieve the best acoustics possible in order to obtain a perfect rendition from different types of bell, amongst which are tubular ones, which generate every note and can be rung by being struck or by injected air, activated by using a keyboard.

01

02

03

04

05

06

08

07

01. THE STAIRS

THE FIRST FLOORS OF THE BELL TOWERS ARE REACHED BY MEANS OF NARROW WINDING STAIRCASES, ONE OF GAUDÍ'S PREFERRED SHAPES, WHO WAS INSPIRED BY NATURE IN ORDER TO CREATE HIS CONSTRUCTIVE STRUCTURES. THESE STAIRS ARRIVE UP TO THE TOWER BALCONIES.

02. THE STAIR STRUCTURE

DUE TO THEIR NARROWNESS, THE STAIRS MAKE THE VISITOR FEEL AS IF HE IS GOING BACK ON HIMSELF. THE REDUCED AREA ALLOWS THE SKIRTING BOARD TO ACT AS A BANNISTER. IN ORDER TO PROVIDE A MORE INTERESTING EFFECT, GAUDÍ MADE THE STAIRS OF EACH PAIR OF BELL TOWERS TURN IN THE OPPOSITE DIRECTION.

02

**THE MESSAGES
ON THE TOWERS**

ON THE BELL TOWER WALLS
THE LATIN WORD 'SANCTUS'
(SAINT) IS REPEATED AND
DECORATED IN WARM COL-
OURFUL TILEWORK, THE
SAME WAY AS THE EXPRES-
SION 'SURSUM CORDA'
(HEARTS ARISE), IN STONE.
ON THE PINNACLES, STONE
BLOCKS OF HEXAGONAL
FORM GENERATE THE
WORDS 'HOSANNA' AND
'EXCELSIS' DECORATED
WITH WHITE CERAMIC
WORK.

Following page

01 TO 03. THE PINNACLES

TOTALLY POLYCHROME, THE
ENDINGS OF THE BELL TOW-
ERS MEASURE 25 METRES
HIGH. ON THEIR BASE IS THE
INSCRIPTION 'HOSANNA
EXCELSIS' (SAFE HIGH UP),
WHILE HIGHER UP A RING
CAN BE MADE OUT, AN EPIS-
COPAL SYMBOL, IN WHOSE
HOLLOW WILL BE PUT THE
LIGHTS THAT WILL ILLUMI-
NATE JESUS' TOWER.

04. PINNACLE DETAIL

GAUDÍ COMBINED MATERI-
ALS, SUCH AS STONE AND
MOSAIC 'TRENCADÍS' WORK,
IN ORDER TO GIVE DIFFER-
ENT GLOSS AND TEXTURES
TO THE PINNACLES.

05. ROSETTE

AT THE BASE OF THE PINNA-
CLE, AT THE END OF THE
BODY OF THE TOWER, EACH
BELL TOWER HAS 12
ROSETTES OF DIFFERENT
COLOURS.

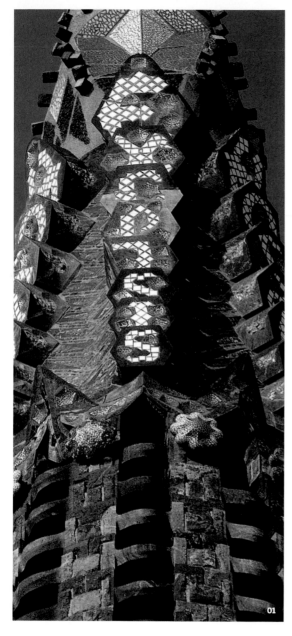

THE TOWER ENDINGS. THE EPISCOPAL ICONS, SUCH AS THE INITIAL OF THE APOSTLE'S NAME TO WHOM EACH BELL TOWER IS DEDICATED, DOMINATE THE PINNACLES' SYMBOLISM, DECORATED WITH VIBRANT COLOUR AND SURROUNDED BY ROUNDED SHAPES IN ORDER HAT THEY CAN BE INTERPRETED FROM A LONG DISTANCE AWAY. THE MOSAIC WORK THAT COVERS THEM IS MADE FROM VENETIAN GLASS FROM MURANO, AN ISLAND KNOWN THROUGHOUT THE WORLD FOR THE ELEGANCE OF ITS GLASSWORK, A HANDICRAFT TRADITION DATING BACK TO THE 15TH CENTURY.

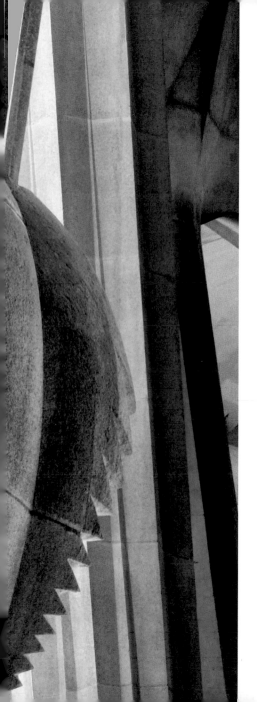

THE TEMPLE NAVES, A PERFECT SPACE FOR MEDITATION AND WORSHIP

NODES
THESE NATURALIST SHAPES MARK THE START
OF THE RAMIFICATION OF THE COLUMNS.

...nature inspired Gaudí to create a revolutionary roof system...

09

THE SPIRITUAL FOREST

Gaudí dedicated 43 years of his career –more than half his life– to the Sagrada Familia project. The experience accumulated during this time, his almost obsessive professional perfectionism and his Christian faith, which grew to such an extent over these decades until transforming into the centre of his existence, converted him into a great expert on liturgy. Above all, the architect wanted Sagrada Familia to be the perfect place for worship and all this depended on structural and decorative considerations. ✑ Gaudí designed a temple of vast dimensions, with five naves and a Latin cross ground plan –one of his scarce concessions to classical canons–, devoting the arrangement of the interior to the exaltation of the universal Church by means of representations of daily prayers and those from the Gospel and epistles that are read out in Sunday mass. All the proportions of the building stem from a basic module of 7.5 by 7.5 metres, which is the distance between the centre of the nave columns. Therefore, the interior length of the temple reaches 90 metres, while its width and height measure 45, half. The crossing arm takes up two thirds of the dimensions of the nave (60 by 30 metres), while the height of the cimborio vault reaches 60 metres, the lateral naves half (30 metres) and the central nave, 45 metres. All of them, multiples of 7.5. ✑ In a first project, in the year 1898, Gaudí thought about erecting the temple in the Gothic style. emulating the great medieval cathedrals. Nonetheless, despite recognising it as an artistic and historic reference, the architect considered the Gothic to be a very imperfect art, given that it used constructive elements that were unable to support themselves. In this first project, in order to avoid the use of buttresses, Gaudí devised very canted arches that could withstand the pressure of the vaults. Nonetheless, this option did not really convince him and as time went on the artist   →

worked on his original method of the calculation of structures, based on experimentation using models to which were applied weights that were proportional to the real load that the arches and columns had to support. But it wasn't until 1924, two years before his death, when he decided to do away with the Gothic system of ribbed vaults and designed a roof with a structure of tree-like columns and hyperboloid vaults unequalled in the history of architecture. ❧ The solution, ideal from the constructive point of view as well as the aesthetic, transforms the temple into a forest of columns that branch out further up, filtering the light that enters through windows and skylights while generating an atmosphere that invites prayer and makes way for transcendence. ❧ In order to raise these columns, Antoni Gaudí considered four different types of materials, according to the weight they had to support: Montjuïc sandstone, granite, basalt and porphyry stone. The architect reserved this last mineral, which was very hard-wearing, for the four thick columns that supported the vault of the largest cimborio, the highest point in the temple's interior, and divided the naves on the far ends into two levels in order to install the choirstands on the upper floor, whose tiers could hold 1,200 choristers in celebrations with a possible congregation of fourteen thousand people.

❧
01. 02 AND 03. INTERIOR OF THE NATIVITY FAÇADE
GAUDÍ LEFT BLOCKS OF STONE WITH BASIC SHAPES IN ORDER THAT THEY WERE SCULPTED ONCE THE NAVE ROOF AND CROSSING ARM WERE FINISHED.

❧
04. INTERIOR OF THE LATERAL WALL
A GALLERY GOES AROUND THE INTERIOR WALLS OF THE TEMPLE, YET TO BE DECORATED WITH THE PLANNED SCULPTURAL ICONOGRAPHY.

04

02

01. THE STONE FOREST
VIEW TOWARDS A SIDE OF
THE TEMPLE VAULTS
WHERE THE RAMIFICATION
OF THE COLUMNS START-
ING FROM THE NODES CAN
BE OBSERVED, ALONG WITH
THE VAULTS MADE FROM
REINFORCED CONCRETE
ON THE LATERAL NAVES
AND, ON THE LOWER PART
OF THE IMAGE, THE UPPER
FLOOR THAT, ON THE FAR
END NAVES, HOLDS THE
STANDS FOR THE CHOIR.

02 AND 03
THE COLUMN NODES
GAUDÍ DEVISED THESE
FORMS IN ORDER TO MARK
THE START OF THE RAMIFI-
CATION OF THE COLUMNS
AND IN THEM DESIGNED
HOLLOWS TO HOLD LIGHTS.

03

THE COLUMNS AND VAULTS

Faithful to the teachings of nature, Gaudí was greatly inspired in the year 1924 to find a solution for the temple roof. The columns, slightly slanting in order to withstand weight better, branched out from numerous transition nodes and concluded in the vaults forming veins similar to those of a palm leaf. The four columns on the intersection between the nave and crossing arm, dedicated to the Evangelists, are the thickest, as they have to hold up the central cimborio. The twelve columns that go around the crossing arm are dedicated to the apostles, while the remaining ones are dedicated to bishops, who continued on with apostles' work. ❧ The interior roof, very light and permeable for the entrance of light, is an original version of the Catalan bricked vault, but based on ceramic tile work on the central nave and reinforced concrete on the sides, instead of traditional and humble brick. ❧ The solidness of the structure allows for the possibility of large zenithal openings that, along with the windows and rose windows in the walls, provide light to the interior in a uniform way. The metallic wire diffusers that Gaudí planned to cover these hollows, such as the stained glass windows designed by Catalan artist Joan Vila-Grau, filter light through in order to achieve, in an enormous space, an ideal atmosphere for recollection and prayer. ❧

THE VAULTS

AZIMUTHAL VIEW OF THE NAVE VAULTS, SUPPORTED BY THE TREE-LIKE COLUMNS THAT BRANCH OUT UP TO 45 METRES HIGH. THE CENTRAL VAULT, BASED ON CERAMIC TILES FOLLOWING THE BRICKED OR CATALAN TECHNIQUE, HAS NUMEROUS SKYLIGHTS TO PROVIDE NATURAL LIGHT TO THE TEMPLE. ON BOTH FAR ENDS OF THE IMAGE STARRED VAULTS ON THE LATERAL NAVES CAN BE OBSERVED, BUILT FROM CONCRETE.

following page

01. ELECTRICAL ILLUMINATION

THE LIGHTS ARE POSITIONED AND DESIGNED TO ILLUMINATE AS NATURAL LIGHT DOES.

02. ILLUMINATION

THE STAINED GLASS WINDOWS, SUCH AS THOSE ON THE PASSION FAÇADE SEEN FROM THE INTERIOR, GIVE WARMTH TO THE NATURAL LIGHT THAT ENTERS THE TEMPLE.

03. CENTRAL VAULT

GREEN COLOURED TRENCADÍS CERAMIC WORK IS INSERTED IN BETWEEN THE ROWS OF TILES THAT MAKE UP THE BRICKED VAULT.

04. THE CROSSING ARM

IMAGE OF A SIDE OF THE CROSSING ARM, ON THE WESTERN SIDE, NEXT TO THE PASSION FAÇADE.

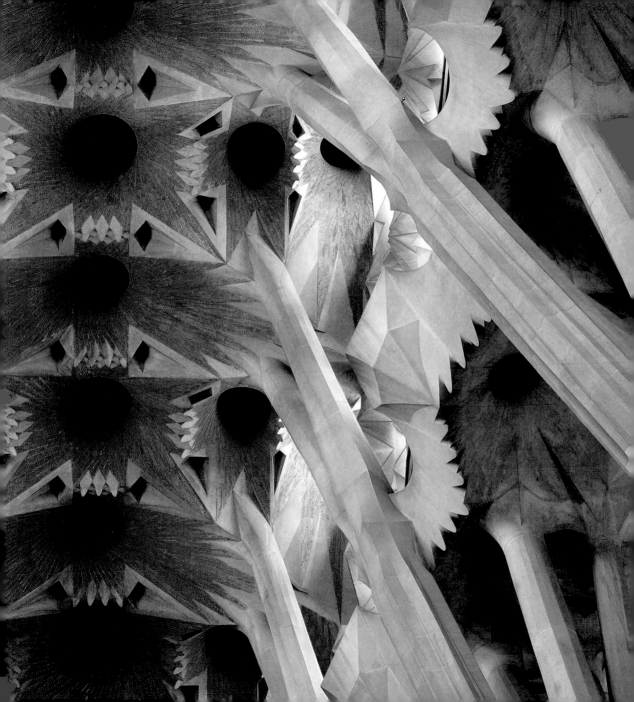

STAINED GLASS WINDOWS. THE CATALAN ARTIST JOAN VILA-GRAU HAS BEEN WORKING SINCE 1999 ON THE DESIGN OF THE STAINED GLASS WINDOWS AND ROSE WINDOWS OF THE SAGRADA FAMILIA, INTERPRETING IN HIS OWN STYLE THE CHROMATIC IDEA DEVISED BY GAUDÍ, WHO SAID THAT "ILLUMINATION MUST BE JUST ENOUGH AND NO MORE, GIVEN THAT IN A TEMPLE RECOLLECTION MUST REIGN". VILA-GRAU DESIGNS THE STAINED GLASS WINDOWS WITH COLD AND WARM COLOURS, AND IN MANY CASES COMBINES BOTH COLOUR SCHEMES TO CREATE SURPRISING EFFECTS.

01

02

03

WALLS AND ROOF

Thanks to the structure devised by Antoni Gaudí, the lateral walls of the temple are freed from the function of supporting weight, which meant that the architect could project much lighter walls and install larger windows and rose windows that would guarantee the temple natural light. In keeping with the artistic maturity of the architect, these different types of openings in the walls underwent an evolution starting from the neo-Gothic style of the hollows found in the crypt to the geometric-naturalist abstraction of the windows on the central nave. ❧ Each one of the stretches of these walls finishes in a triangular decorative ending on whose vertex the sculptor Etsuro Sotoo carved baskets of fruit –symbol of the riches that the Holy Spirit scattered on Earth– covered with, like the bell tower pinnacles, vibrant polychrome Venetian mosaic work. ❧ The outer roof of the temple, which has to provide protection for the interior bricked vault, is made up of a series of pyramids that are similar to –in smaller dimensions– the shapes of the cimborios projected by Gaudí, and are topped with a lantern and a lamp, seventy metres high, twenty-five metres above the mentioned interior vault. In order to make it as light as possible, this exterior roof is planned to use Montjuïc sandstone, which is not as dense as granite. ❧

SYMBOLIC MESSAGES ON THE LATERAL WALLS. BETWEEN THE WINDOWS OF THE EXTERIOR WALLS OF THE TEMPLE, ON SOME HELICOIDAL COLUMNS, ENGRAVED IN STONE, AND LATER HIGHLIGHTED WITH PAINT, LATIN WORDS SUCH AS 'THUS' (INCENSE), 'MYRRHAM' (MYRRH) AND 'AURUM' (GOLD), REFERRING TO THE GIFTS MADE BY THE THREE WISE KINGS TO JESUS AT HIS BIRTH IN BETHLEHEM, AND OTHERS IN THE CATALAN LANGUAGE, LIKE 'ORACIÓ (PRAYER) ', 'SACRIFICI' AND 'ALMOINA' (CHARITY), WHICH REFER TO THE QUALITIES A GOOD CHRISTIAN MUST POSSESS.

🙵 **THE FOUNDING SAINTS.** IN ALL THE EXTERIOR MONUMENT OF THE TEMPLE –THE APSE AND THE TWO LATERAL WALLS OF THE NAVES–, ON THE UPPER PART OF EACH ONE OF THE STRETCHES OF WINDOWS, GAUDÍ PROPOSED PUTTING IMAGES OF THE FOUNDING SAINTS OF THE MAIN RELIGIOUS ORDERS, SUCH AS TERESA DE JESUS (CARMELITES), FRANCISCO DE ASSISI (FRANCISCANS), SAN BENITO DE NURSIA (BENEDICTINES), SAN BERNARDO DE CLARAVAL (INSTIGATOR OF THE CISTERCIAN ORDER), SAN JUAN BOSCO (SALESIANS), AND SAN IGNACIO DE LOYOLA (JESUITS).

10

THE SIMPLE YET INGENIOUS STRUCTURE OF THE SCHOOLROOMS

THE ROOF

THE UNDULATING ROOF PROVIDES LIGHTNESS AND RESISTANCE TO THE BUILDING.

...its warped roof is considered to be one of Gaudí's masterpieces...

LEFT
THE MAIN ENTRANCE TO
THE SCHOOLROOMS,
WITH THE LAMP AND THE
SIGN, PAINTED ON MOR-
TAR. BEHIND THIS BUILD-
ING THE PASSION
FAÇADE'S TOWERS CAN
BE MADE OUT.

BELOW
ONE OF THE THREE
ROOMS IN THE SCHOOL-
ROOMS IS EQUIPPED WITH
FURNITURE AND OBJECTS,
SUCH AS THIS LAMP,
FROM THE ORIGINAL
CLASSROOMS.

THE SUBLIME HUMBLENESS OF BRICK

Primary and secondary education were one of the strategic points in the plan of action that the Association of Devotees, promoter association of the Sagrada Familia, had set itself. The neighbourhood where the temple was being built, popularly known as El Poblet (the village), was an area of modest properties where many children did not receive any type of education at all. In 1908, Father Gil Parés, first chaplain-custodian of the Sagrada Familia crypt, suggested to Gaudí the planning and construction on the land of an inexpensive building –its location had to be provisional– that would serve as an education centre for the neighbourhood and the children of the labourers that worked on the temple. The architect got down to work and designed a minimalist building, comprised of just one floor, built from solid brick –including the roof– and without any decoration. Nonetheless the simplicity of these plans and the contrast of dimensions and quality of the materials to the enormous temple alongside do not take away an inch of ingenuity from this work, which counts as one of the most representative works of Gaudí. It is a long building, without arrises, with two partition walls inside that generate three classrooms which can hold up to 150 pupils in total. The toilets occupy two small rooms at the far ends, with access from the interior and from the patio. The walls are made up of two layers of brick erected with quick cement. The laying of bricks is surprisingly simple. The bricks are positioned vertically –in order to permit the developing curve of the façade–, on their larger side, as in partition walls and bricked vaults– and in rows, with continuous joins. Three iron pillars support a master beam of the same material which in turn holds up small wooden beams. The great secret for this simple framework is held in the conoid structure designed by Gaudí,

→

which generates a warped roof that is light and resistant and allows for the immediate draining away of rain water. Moreover, this rational and innovative solution greatly impressed Swiss architect Le Corbusier, one of the most influential architects of the 20th century, on a visit to Barcelona in 1928. ❧ Inaugurated in the autumn of 1909, the schoolrooms were pioneering in the application of so-called active pedagogy, a very progressive educational method characterized by its respect towards the pupil as a person, at a time when corporal punishment was the norm in educational institutions. Construction cost 9.000 pesetas (which is around 54 euros). Gaudí is said to have paid from his own pocket due to his affinity with the ideas of Father Parés, with whom he had an excellent relationship. ❧ Despite the temporary nature with which they were planned, the schoolrooms were used for their educative purpose up until the 1980's and in 2002 they were moved, as they took up an area facing Mallorca Street destined for the temple naves. Their reconstruction next to the Passion façade meant that more secrets of their rationalist construction could be discovered. Nowadays, the schoolrooms hold the didactic room of the museum of the Sagrada Familia, with a reproduction of Gaudí's workshop and some of the models and plans made by the architect. ❧

THE SCHOOLROOMS IN THE 1920'S
IMAGE OF THE ORIGINAL LOCATION OF THE SCHOOLROOMS, PARALLEL TO MALLORCA STREET. IN 1936, SHORTLY AFTER THE START OF THE CIVIL WAR, A GROUP OF PEOPLE SET FIRE TO THE BUILDING, WHICH WAS LATER RESTORED WHEN THE STRUGGLE CAME TO AN END. IN THE YEAR 2002 THE SCHOOLROOMS WERE MOVED TO THEIR PRESENT LOCATION.

Following page
01. THE CLASSROOM
REPLICA OF THE PERIOD WITH TABLES, DESKS AND ORIGINAL LAMPS IN ONE OF THE FORMER CLASSROOMS OF THE BUILDING.

02. THE ROOF
CLOSE UP OF THE WARPED STRUCTURE OF THE ROOF, GENERATED BY SMALL WOODEN BEAMS THAT ARE SUPPORTED BY A MASTER BEAM. THE ROOF, LIKE THE INTERIOR AND EXTERIOR WALLS, IS MADE FROM SOLID BRICK.

03. GAUDÍ'S WORKSHOP
A REPRODUCTION OF THE ARCHITECT'S TABLE IS SHOWN IN THE SCHOOLROOMS AS PART OF THE SAGRADA FAMILIA MUSEUM'S DIDACTIC ROOM.

04. THE WINDOWS
THE LINTELS ON THE WINDOWS ARE THE ONLY PART OF THE BUILDING CONSTRUCTED WITH BRICKS PLACED ON THEIR SIDES, IN ORDER TO ACHIEVE SOLIDNESS AND STABILITY.

THE EXPIATORY TEMPLE OF THE SAGRADA FAMILIA
THE CREATION WHICH ANTONI GAUDÍ DEDICATED HIS ENTIRE LIFE TO

PUBLISHED BY
© DOS DE ARTE EDICIONES, S.L., BARCELONA, 2009

TEXTS
MANAGING DIRECTORS:
CARLOS GIORDANO AND NICOLÁS PALMISANO
REDACTION: RICARD REGÀS
TRANSLATIONS:
CERYS GIORDANO JONES AND DYLAN GIORDANO JONES
© DOS DE ARTE EDICIONES, S.L., BARCELONA, 2009

PHOTOGRAPHS
AUTHORS: CARLOS GIORDANO AND NICOLÁS PALMISANO
© DOS DE ARTE EDICIONES, S.L., BARCELONA, 2009

PHOTOGRAPHS INTERIOR OF TEMPLE AND MUSEUM
AUTHORS: CARLOS GIORDANO AND NICOLÁS PALMISANO
© CARLOS GIORDANO, NICOLÁS PALMISANO AND JUNTA
   CONSTRUCTORA DEL TEMPLE EXPIATORI DE LA SAGRADA
   FAMÍLIA, BARCELONA, 2009

PHOTOGRAPHS AND DRAWINGS FROM ARCHIVE
PAGES: 009, 010, 012, 013, 014, 015, 016, 017, 022, 023, 038,
049, 051, 060, 088, 094 (2), 106, 108, 109, 111, 117, 134 AND 156.
© JUNTA CONSTRUCTORA DEL TEMPLE EXPIATORI
   DE LA SAGRADA FAMÍLIA

ACKNOWLEDGMENTS
· JUNTA CONSTRUCTORA DEL TEMPLE EXPIATORI
   DE LA SAGRADA FAMÍLIA
· ARXIU DEL TEMPLE

FIRST EDITION 2009

ISBN
978-84-96783-47-8

DEPÓSITO LEGAL
B-23.501-2009

PRINTED IN SPAIN

www.dosdearte.com

Using the code you will be
able to download extra material, visiting the "Download
zone" on our web page.

CCY3511JHH

DOS De
aRTe
EDICIONES

www.dosdearte.com
info@dosdearte.com

Temple Expiatori de la
SAGRADA FAMÍLIA

WITH THE COLLABORATION
OF THE JUNTA CONSTRUCTORA
DEL TEMPLE EXPIATORI
DE LA SAGRADA FAMILIA